THE PROPHET'S TOOTHBRUSH

poems by

Elia Hohauser-Thatcher

Finishing Line Press
Georgetown, Kentucky

THE PROPHET'S TOOTHBRUSH

Copyright © 2021 by Elia Hohauser-Thatcher
ISBN 978-1-64662-529-1 First Edition
All rights reserved under International and Pan-American Copyright Conventions. No part of this book may be reproduced in any manner whatsoever without written permission from the publisher, except in the case of brief quotations embodied in critical articles and reviews.

ACKNOWLEDGMENTS

I am grateful to the editors of the following publications, in which these poems first appeared or are forthcoming (some in slightly different versions or with different titles):

Fearsome Critters: "Mirror," "Ode to Kylo Ren"
Heron Tree: "Still Life"
Soul-Lit: "The Prophet"
The Maine Review: "Poseidon"
The Offbeat: "King Jellyfish"
Up North Lit: "Uncle Eric teaches me to fish"
Weatherbeaten Lit: "Landmark," "Last Star in the Universe"

All author proceeds will be donated to HAVEN of Oakland County, an organization that provides shelter, counseling, advocacy, and educational programming for survivors of domestic violence and sexual assault.

Publisher: Leah Huete de Maines
Editor: Christen Kincaid
Cover Art: Anthony Brazeau
Author Photo: Shelby Newsom
Cover Design: Elizabeth Maines McCleavy

Order online: www.finishinglinepress.com
also available on amazon.com

Author inquiries and mail orders:
Finishing Line Press
PO Box 1626
Georgetown, Kentucky 40324
USA

Table of Contents

Landmark 1

A Man's Body 2

Divorce 3

Uncle Eric teaches me to fish 4

My father's pipe 5

Island 6

Still Life 7

Labatt Blues 8

Sermon 9

Trinity 10

Painting my toenails 11

King Jellyfish 12

Poseidon 13

The Prophet 14

Ode to Kylo Ren 15

Root Cellar 16

You're moving slower than molasses in January! 17

Intimacy 18

Alcoholic 19

Last Star in the Universe 20

Mirror 21

One Month 22

The Prophet's Toothbrush 23

Landmark

Mom soars down I-75, Rubber Soul in the tape deck,
says, *don't date downriver girls*. Metallic stench
of industry corrodes their skin, their teeth like old books.

Disease, another synonym for sex. *Blame Detroit* she says.
All that pollution dribbles into their veins, arteries corrode,
Ford's oil a burning river. *They're dirty* she says.

I cheat on my first girlfriend with a downriver girl.
I bike through rain on a moonless night, burst
in on a backdoor sleepover. Our hips align
as I spill into 6 a.m. dawn, strangle a car horn's cry.

Out the window of our VW van, mom flicks
a cigarette butt, unaware of my future shame.
I-75 is the passing of time unwound.
Sin, a landmark to pass.

A Man's Body

I leave the shower, wrap a towel
around my waist and pass stepdad
in the hallway. His black-ringed
stare, straw beard, blue button-up
the color of his eyes.
You have a man's body now.

A man's body. Small dollop
of stomach forming, curly hairs
dripping from chin to pelvis,
shoulders pulled in iron vice,
tulip-bulb fists, hot ash of bravado
in my cheeks, belt in my left hand notched
clumsily with a butter knife.

Mom arranges herself
between us, tries to lay a wreath
of chrysanthemums on my brow,
peels stepdad's gaze away
like rind from an orange.
Jay's just saying you look healthy.

I sneak into my bedroom to heap
on boxers, jeans, a blue sweatshirt.
Try to cover the violence.

Divorce

In 2011, Mom chips away colors with a thumbnail.
Green stem stains her reclusive fingers.

The impossible choice: scrape or whitewash.
Her knuckles brush clavicle in nervous itch.

In 1991, Dad painted lilies on mom's wall.
The day before, his roommate dangled

him from a window by the ankles, worm-lips
crooned over the quad: *you dirty Jew, you dirty Jew.*

Mom found him, red-faced with his brush,
caressed Dad's clavicle with knuckles,

stroked his curly hair. He wept
greens, yellows, whites onto the floor,

coalesced into the color of lilies.
Ankles burned, clavicles itched. They spilled

paint, pretended for a while, as crows
sang of their coupling from the windowsill:

Tell her she's crazy. Call him a kike.
Have a child.

Uncle Eric teaches me to fish

as pike and bluegill tread
the width of Little Torch.

His thumbs, thick padded scars
from lips uncounted, pull
taut the knot. He pricks
worms with silver hooks,
hands covered in silt.

Perched near the bow, we survey
a sodden shore. Loons skim
the blue opacity, gnats weave
patterns, breeze pulls
waterlilies and crushed pine needles.

Wandering half-father.
Lets me drink Sierra Nevadas,
ramble among conifers, vault
over the pink moon.

Feter. Mentor.
Wears mustaches,
patience, laughter—
euphonies of Ellsworth.

He lights a cigarillo and turns
the motor to life, winks
as the smoke rises like astral dust:
Nothing better than this.

My father's pipe

is nothing remarkable
a thing of utility   blemished
clunky wood   smoke
caresses the bowels of your cheeks

primal sludge
of smoked tobacco writhes
that burned incense   rubbed raw
by chafe of fire

i have one now and again
just as my father does   a mark
my inheritance
fingers yellowed from caress

him in the molten gray back room
of detroit's penthouse strip club

me pacing in front   no decision made
my kosher lips on tiger's eye
plastic tip   greedy

girlfriends and wives at home
their absent kisses
sting   our addiction

i suck in all the smoky guilt
the infidelity like emphysema
lung cancer

the lie i tell myself
as i walk inside
the lie i tell myself
as i light up

only the habit will kill you

Island

i kiss my girlfriend open-mouthed,
mostly-hard. her fleshy tongue
is too easily bitten,
so i latch on & lock my jaw.

grandpa backhands,
dad shoves & smashes appliances,
stepdad chooses fists. their lack
of originality goes unnoticed.

i chew so hard on chicken bones
they splinter & the marrow
clings to my teeth. so little pressure
for cartilage to crack.

we are as empty as the sixth beer, a noose,
an island in an ocean. serrated fish hooks,
incisors & deflated footballs stacked
higher than our skulls.

i see the vacant land, trash piled high
& don't know what to plant.

Still Life

Two red anjou pears
cannot possibly seek to fill
this clay bowl   my mother
gave me.

I have let them sit
for so long, only today
I wanted one for breakfast.

My fingers outstretched, they
pushed through   weak skin
and I felt the viscid pulp
inside.

The sweet
          rotted flesh.

Labatt Blues

Daffodil pilsner, carbonated acid crutch.
Sticky two sips at the bottom of the bottle.
Replaced Stroh's in '85 after Ford's mechanics
found wood shavings in the brew.
We don't need bootleggers to smuggle
this Canadian rotgut. Our stepfathers demand
navy-colored vessels, just as we will,
the replaceable drinking-class.
We binge ourselves to sleep.

Patterns of maple leaf bottles guzzled
into returnables, some Lions broadcast
screaming from a big screen teevee.
Our mothers, beaten into silence,
gray cotton sheets on a California King,
room to rest miles away.
We destroy ourselves to sleep.

Sermon

Remember not to talk
about anything that hurts.
In fact, it's best to keep
your mouth shut all the time,
perhaps sewn closed by iris petals.
Now, bow your head,
pretend everything's fine.
Pretend the first thing you notice
isn't the shape of the body,
pretend you aren't ogling
the woman in the white dress,
pretend she was asking for your gaze,
pretend your dad doesn't live
for Bazookie's Strip Club in Detroit,
pretend your stepdad didn't bash
your mom's head into a wall,
pretend you don't want to pummel
his face until he shatters
like a stained-glass window,
pretend you don't want to demand,
red knuckles raised:
Why?

Don't think about your ancestors
who burned witches in the wilderness
circling Boston,
don't think about sleeping around
behind your girlfriend's back,
blond pubic hair on your jeans,
don't think about the buck killed
from a distance and left to rot,
the picture taken with his antlers
in your rough hands—
how you grinned, so strong, so proud
you showed the picture off at school.
Don't you feel like a man now?
Don't you feel like a man?

Trinity
Barry County, Michigan

Mom drives. One painted foot
out the window, heavy breeze
passes through her toes.

Sugar maples unfold on either side
of the highway. They curl—
clutches of ochre in autumn sky.

Dad sleeps. The gentle sway
of Sounds of Silence, his heartbeat,
echoes through gray polyester seat.

Farms rise to my eyes. Rows
of corn, fallen browned maypoles.
The scent of manure
savory and sickening.

We ride toward the center
of the sun as it sets on this
fragile embrace: Mother,
Father and Son.

Hills cut by dirt roads
and stop signs. Rivers limpid,
littered with sharp stones.

Doors slam as shadows lengthen,
footsteps echo into pavement.
Our journey together ends.

Painting my toenails

The ritual of it, that subtle
destruction of perception.

You are pink. Lips
of the first boy I kissed

under bedcovers in Toledo,
crickets purring in the window.

You are hidden. Crushed
beneath sweaty wool socks,

a brightness strangled. No one
believes me when I tell them.

Impossible, they whistle through
their teeth. *Your feet are dirty.*

How many men have you fucked?
Stonewall Rebels laugh in my face.

Have you even suffered for it?
Another girlfriend weeps.

My toenails shine, so pink.
I keep my socks on.

King Jellyfish

My ass sinks lower
than the benthic zone
and I am Jellyfish-Man.
Arms gesticulate, voice becomes a slurp.
                        I call this the wet noodle.
Roll my abdomen, bend
at the knee,
I flex, poplock&drop,
shake it
like a polaroid picture.
The dance floor becomes
my jellyfish fiefdom, friends
are subjects admonished: *No,*
                first to the left, then to the right!
I tie up
invisible lassoes, haul in
a boy, a girl, another boy
until I'm exhausted by my excellence.
I cool off in the hunched over night.
Unwashed masses surround me, neon green anemones.
Electricity sparkles on my forehead
as snowflakes anoint, coronation
of the jellyfish king.

Nobles flank me, we tidal wave
into a gold Chevy Impala.
In the backseat, I'm a generous ruler.
Flash a five-dollar bill, wink.
                      Vassals, who wants curly fries?

Poseidon

My father demonstrated
his power under the YMCA
shower head, arms sharpened

into points. Water rushed over
fins, down fingertips
in jets.

At bedtime, he rocked me,
a ship on calm seas as we
sang the old songs.

When he grew archaic—hurricanes.
Kitchen chairs thrown, explosions
into kindling. Blue sky abused

into bruised maroon. I would leave
offerings at his altar: comic books,
drowned gulls, mugs of saltwater.

When danger passed, we swam
together, floated on ocean waves.
He always said: *Son*

when I am with you, nothing
will ever hurt, and all
I could do was believe.

The Prophet

First, I came to be, and thought of a lotus flower:
Fuchsia petals folded back, unspoiled flower.

Among the stenches of my Pittsburgh bus stop, I smell semen
on the wind. The Bartlett Pear Tree flowers.

Dad makes me breakfast, toast cut up in quarters
covered in cinnamon, sugar, butter. Conditions of flour.

On crosses, robbers bow their heads, adorned with thorns.
Their passion brings Mary to tears, waters the flowers.

Autumn blooms, and from the oak leaves underfoot
comes the scent of mom's patchouli, wilting earth flowers.

I am a prophet of the iron book. A crude, misspelled Elijah.
My parents crushed *j* and *h*, stemmed my dripping flower.

Ode to Kylo Ren

> *"I'll destroy her. And you. And all of it."*
> —Kylo Ren, Star Wars: The Last Jedi

I can relate. Hair dark and wavy, dressed in black.
You spat those words to audience laughter:
What a whiny boy. Not me.

Transfixed at a midnight showing, popcorn bag empty,
I nodded. Who hasn't yearned to destroy
the world and remake it
in their image?

There's nothing to level here, Kylo.
You're not alone anymore.
I am just like you.

Face me as a mirror image, striplings forced
to settle. Come, sit next to me, run
your strong hands

through my prematurely graying hair. Part me
down the middle. Kiss me.

Root Cellar

Obscured by black-eyed Susans,
two apple trees bend—lovers
entwined in rigor mortis.
Wooden door, rounded to fit the frame.
Like the parents' bedroom door when they had sex,
once a week. Boy, hand on the doorknob,
too afraid to enter—*No, not now.*

Remember: Apples. Apples growing green,
speckled with brown dots. So sweet,
the jaw reproduces saliva and locks
this door, their door is locked.
Behind, cucumbers and beets pickling,
dead and slick in vinegar.

You're moving slower than molasses in January!

Mom shouts
through my teenage years as I am glued
to my bed again and doing my best to remember the algorithm
for giving a shit about high school. Her folksy Michigan saying
yields minute wisdoms: Molasses, for the amber drip
concentrated to sweeten dark mornings.
January, for how the brown goop freezes
in the bottle and stays so still.

This is forever, I know it. A search party
for answers in my bed of silt, four cobalt walls of perennial twilight,
the scratchy hardwood floors.
Mom knows it, too. Ice settles on her roots and she gets stuck.
Some weekend afternoons I find her sprawled 'til two beneath
that greenleaf comforter, snoring louder than a wolverine.
That's why she hollers from the living room,
never comes to check. She knows what's going on.

Intimacy

War has come to our basement.
Under the false wood panels,
under swaying saffron banners—tatters
above a child's crib. Fluorescent lights
illuminate a knitted blanket that dresses
her legs, the blotchy violet spots.
Her ruddy cheeks flutter.
My mother dreams, confesses: *son,
abuse is intimate, almost like making love.*
Empty bottles mewl in the darkened room,
my stepfather wraps his fingers
around her throat, whispers *I love you*
until the silent blood vessels burst.
His mouth slobbers in ecstasy, thirst.

Alcoholic

I.
The compulsion to slip amber past my lips
gestated. My mom gulped bottles of Cabernet
to drown my uncle's corpse. My grandfather,
tongue wet with gin, painted a fence naked.
My great-grandfather went blind from bathtub hooch.

I despise these veins, these lips, this family
that strapped me to a hospital bed. So drunk
I forgot the concrete, the fall.
My arm, face and liver scarred. Internal ticking
of history, ends healing on their ends. My end?

II.
I am a stepdad; I am four DUI's. With effort,
I drink fears into silence, willfully suspend disbelief
until my yellow fingers curl into fists.
Then I sit still, fuming in a La-Z-Boy.
Only rise to grab a whiskey, yell, or swing.

At fifty-five, I am dead. My yellow fists clench
into dust, my tombstone bears a Bukowski quote.
Don't Try. The day I die, my fourteen-year-old stepson embarks,
sneaks Labatts from the fridge at my wake.

Last Star in the Universe

I was 23 when I became a man, washing
my mom's blood from the wall
where my stepdad smashed
her head in, the black hole still visible.

I became a man when my hands folded
mom's laundry, rinsed her dishes,
dressed the peeling scabs on her back.
When I heard her repeat for the twentieth time:
*Then he got the scissors and said
if you're a dyke, I'm gonna give you
a dyke haircut.*

I became a man when the supernova
of my anger exploded into a million red dwarves,
when the constellations faded
into lifeless pink light pollution,
when I dumped her cigarette butts in the trash
and rinsed out Labatt Blue bottles,
when I slammed those bottles down
just to watch something break—
when I took the last star in the universe,
ran it under tepid water,
and watched it dissolve like Alka-Seltzer
in the palm of my hand.

Mirror

I'm getting better at lying
still on my mattress, hands tucked
under my thighs. At consuming
reruns with alarming pace
and whispering my curtains closed.
At playing taciturn while my fitted sheet
winks off the corner.
Getting better at being alone,
at ignoring texts, turning
the light off, wearing down
my gums with a toothbrush
before I fall asleep.
Getting better at taking
deep breaths, at scrolling through
Facebook, Instagram, Twitter, until
my thumbs turn into chuck.
Getting better at donning
the mask before I post
a status, picture, tweet.
Scarlet, with a forked tongue,
thick hair the color of seaweed.
Getting better at glaring
into the mirror, that wooden face someone
I no longer recognize.

One Month

Styrofoam cups packed
with brown discipline,
I fantasize for a sip and wake up
sober with a bloody nose. My heroes
are men with fault-line faces, tectonic
plates shifting post-earthquake.
They clamber to tell stories of misdeeds.
My turn: *Hello, my name is who cares
and I'm an alcoholic. Once, I drank
so much I pissed in a dresser.*
Acrid grounds are boiling over,
sizzle on a hot plate, hiss between stories.
Brother, may I bum a square?
Outside the church
we smoke them (one addiction
at a time). The effort of taking a drag
exhausting, *I'd love a beer right now,
yespleasethankyou.* I flick my butt,
return to God's basement, return
to the holy circle of plastic chairs.
One month sober and I demand calories,
excuses for acting like an asshole,
warm glow of the neon Budweiser sign.
Instead, I'm here under fluorescent lights
with pock-marked angels who cry
when you poke them. *I drank so much
I hrut semoen, I drnak os mushc
I*

The Prophet's Toothbrush

Misspelled Elijah, speaker of the iron book,
you should feel guilt. When was the last time
you sat in the dentist's chair?
I can see the black sickle of cavity
on your front tooth, your gums recede
from being too vigorous with me.
Friends think you quit smoking
but I know better, that post-breakup
Pall Mall breath. I know you bite down hard
on the filter, gum it all up with your spit.
How will you spread God's word now?
You gaze upon the false icon—her stuck-out-tongue
likeness on your cell phone. From the bathroom sink
I see you curled up on tiled floor,
becoming one with the void.

Remember your lessons. Jesus cleansed
Jerusalem's temple of greed and profit.
St. Margaret, swallowed by Satan, escaped
alive with her cross. You must twice defy.
Please. Go to the dentist. I can't be the only one
to help you scourge yourself of plaque and sin.
Throw that pack of Pall Malls in the trash,
delete those pictures off your phone,
and for God's sake, floss.

Additional Acknowledgements

A heartfelt thank you to Mel DeStefano, Amanda Kay Oaks, Kerryn McMurdo, Walter Lucken IV, and Isaac Pickell, who read this manuscript at various stages and gave me crucial feedback.

A thank you to Chatham University's wonderful MFA program, where many of these poems took shape. Special love to Cedric Rudolph, my brother in poetry. My thanks, also, to the women who helped shape me at Chatham: Heather McNaugher, Sheila Squillante, Sheryl St. Germain, and Sarah Shotland.

Thanks to Mom, the strongest woman I know. Thanks to Dad, the giver of secrets. Thanks to Alex Gilman, who helps me be a better man.

Finally, greatest thanks to Shelby Newsom, who put these poems in the right order. I love you more every day.

Elia Hohauser-Thatcher received his MFA from Chatham University, where he served as the Margaret Whitford Fellow. His work has appeared in *Great Lakes Review, The Maine Review, The Offbeat, Lunch, Fearsome Critters, The Detroit Socialist, Up North Lit, The Northridge Review, Gyroscope Review, Soul-Lit, Weatherbeaten Literature, Heron Tree, Around Poetry,* and in anthologies such as *Secret Destinations, Weaving the Terrain* and *States of the Union.* Currently, he is pursuing his PhD in Rhetoric & Composition and teaching at Wayne State University. He runs FlowerHouse Creative Writing Group out of his home in Hamtramck, Michigan.

www.ingramcontent.com/pod-product-compliance
Lightning Source LLC
LaVergne TN
LVHW041522070426
835507LV00012B/1765